Autumn Activities

A Change of Seasons

Autumn is a time of dramatic change in many places. Children can see that as summer passes to autumn, leaves often change color. They can also feel the change of weather as mornings grow colder in some places. Because of cooler weather, the activities of life change for people, as well as for some animals. Animals prepare for winter; some hibernate or migrate while others store food or grow extra fur. There are celebrations at this time of year; some focus on giving thanks for the bounty from the land. It is also a busy time as many people prepare for the cold weather and winter holidays to come.

Activities

- Collect leaves, comparing variations in color and design.
- To decorate and brighten the walls make posters about autumn celebrations and seasonal changes.
- Many animals prepare for winter by hibernation or migration. Find and read picture books that have examples of these animals.
- Make a chart about animals that hibernate and one about those who migrate.
- Make a table centerpiece with an autumn theme. Arrange small pumpkins, gourds, and leaves on a paper plate. Tuck the leaves between and under the vegetables.
- Commemorate United Nations' Day on October 24. Choose some member countries to learn about. Provide books or travel information about these countries. Have each child choose a country and draw the country's flag on the front of a plain index card. On the back, write the name of the country and a few facts about that country.

- Make paper bag masks of famous people recognized in the autumn months. Use construction paper, felt pieces, and crayons to decorate them. Examples of historical or literary figures include Columbus, Squanto, a Pilgrim, Johnny Appleseed, or Jack Frost. Children can have fun wearing the masks and pretending to be those people

Bibliography

Devlin, Wendy. *Cranberry Autumn.* Four Winds, 1992.

Sweninger, Ann. *Autumn Days.* Viking, 1991.

Turner, Ann Warren. *Rainflowers.* Harper Collins, 1993.

Van Allsburg, Chris. *The Stranger.* Houghton Mifflin, 1986.

Zolotow, Charlotte. *Say It!* Green Willow Books, 1980.

Say It!

Author: Charlotte Zolotow

Publisher: Green Willow Books, 1980.

(Available in Canada, Gage Distributors; UK, International Book Distributors; AUS, Kirby Book Company)

Summary: A little girl and her mother go for a walk on a beautiful, blustery autumn day. As they go along, they see many sights. They see a black kitten and many colorful leaves fluttering in the breeze and crunching under their feet. They come to a pond, like a mirror reflecting the autumn colors that abound, and they walk by a hillside with cattle grazing. They meet a big friendly dog and walk by a babbling brook.

As they go along, the little girl wants her mother to "say it," that is, *I love you.* The mother playfully ignores the little girl's requests and says something else. When they get home, the mother finally says "I love you." She explains that she had been saying that all along in many ways.

Connecting Activities:

- Discuss and list the signs of autumn found in your area.

- Then, read the book to your children. Ask about the signs of autumn they see in the book as the little girl and her mother walk.

- Discuss the bond between the little girl and her mother. What good feelings are shown? Ask the children about their bonds with and feelings for another person. What are some ways to show friendship, love and caring?

- Look at magazines to find pictures showing friendship. Cut out and glue these pictures on a piece of construction paper. Title these **FRIENDSHIP** or **CARING,** etc. Laminate the collages and use them as place mats for Thanksgiving dinner or make sets for special gifts.

- Create autumn bookmarks. Cut construction paper into 3" x 8" (7.5 cm x 20 cm) strips. Draw autumn pictures on these and title them. For instance, if a child draws leaves of various colors he or she might write **"Changing Leaves of Autumn."**

- Elicit from the children some feelings that are common to all people, and then ask them why they think people have these feelings.

- Write the mother's responses to the girl's questions on a piece of poster board or tagboard. How do her words *show* love without actually *stating* the words of love?

Scenes from Say It!

Directions:

- Duplicate this page on bond paper or card stock.

- Think about the story *Say It!*. Color these pictures of things the little girl and her mother see on their walk.

- On the line under the pictures, write the words from the mother's answers as they encounter each new autumn scene.

- Cut out the pictures and staple them together to make a small booklet. Make and decorate covers for your own book. Use white construction paper cut to 3" x 4" (7.5 cm by 10 cm).

the black cat

1._____

the little pond

2._____

fluff of milkweed

3._____

floating clouds

4._____

their house

5._____

the little girl

6._____

Autumn Celebrations

Holidays in this season are often about celebrating the harvest of the fruits of the land and family togetherness. They also honor those who settled the New World, braving perilous voyages in search of riches and religious freedom.

Holidays and Activities

Columbus Day

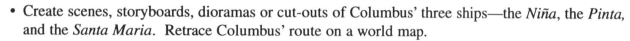

Columbus landed in the New World on October 12, 1492. Most likely, he landed on the island of San Salvador. Columbus Day celebrates his voyage of discovery. It also recognizes the overcoming of great odds because of determination and belief. In the United States, it is recognized on the second Monday of October.

- Create scenes, storyboards, dioramas or cut-outs of Columbus' three ships—the *Niña*, the *Pinta*, and the *Santa Maria*. Retrace Columbus' route on a world map.
- Research life on board Columbus' ships. Present an imaginary interview with Columbus or a member of his crew. Ask about hardships, the food, the long months at sea, and the excitement of discovering a new place. Ask advice for future explorers, such as astronauts exploring space.
- Find out if Columbus Day is celebrated in different countries. Is the day recognized in Central America or the Dominican Republic? Does Columbus' home town of Genoa, Italy, celebrate this holiday?

Halloween

- Halloween is celebrated on October 31. In the United States, children dress in costumes and eat special treats.
- Design your own costumes. Use old clothing and hats to create your costumes.
- The pumpkin is also a part of this day. People carve human-like faces on pumpkins as a part of celebrating Halloween.

- See who can make the most words from HALLOWEEN and give a prize to the person who writes the most in a certain time limit. Some examples are *wall, heel, lane, new*.

Thanksgiving

- In the United States, Thanksgiving is celebrated the fourth Thursday in November. This is to commemorate the Pilgrims who settled Plymouth Colony. They had a feast with the people who helped them survive the first year in the New World.
- Study the Plymouth Pilgrims. Did they go to school? How did they learn? How did they help their parents? What games did they play? What was life like on the *Mayflower* and in Plymouth?
- Make a recipe book of turkey treats. Find ten interesting ways to serve turkey. Write them on index cards. Write a title page using another index card. Fasten the cards together by punching holes in the upper lefthand corners and then inserting paper fasteners in the holes. Give these to parents or other special adults.

A Mini-Book About Autumn

This and the following page are meant to be a mini-book about autumn. Pages one to six can be done at the same time. Pages seven and eight must be done over a one-week time period. Answer the questions and then color or draw the picture for each page. Cut the pages out. Punch a hole out on the left side of each page and put the pages together in order by the numbers. Tie them together with a 10-12" (25–30 cm) piece of string. You may also staple pages.

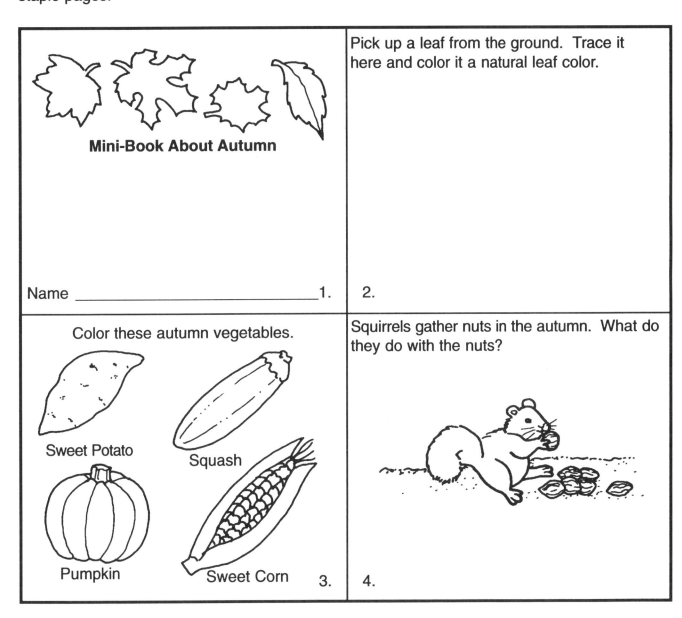

Mini-Book About Autumn

Name _____ 1.

Pick up a leaf from the ground. Trace it here and color it a natural leaf color.

2.

Color these autumn vegetables.

Sweet Potato

Squash

Pumpkin

Sweet Corn 3.

Squirrels gather nuts in the autumn. What do they do with the nuts?

4.

Some animals hibernate in the winter. The bear is one of them.

5.

Draw and color your favorite fall scene.

6.

The days are getting cooler and cooler. Record the temperature where you live each day for a week.

Day	Date	Temp.
Sunday		
Monday		
Tuesday		
Wednesday		
Thursday		
Friday		
Saturday		

7.

In the autumn, days grow shorter. Over seven days, record the date and the time it becomes dark.

Date	Time

8.

Autumn Leaves

Activity:

Some leaves change color in autumn. You may see red, orange, yellow, or golden brown leaves on the trees or ground during this season.

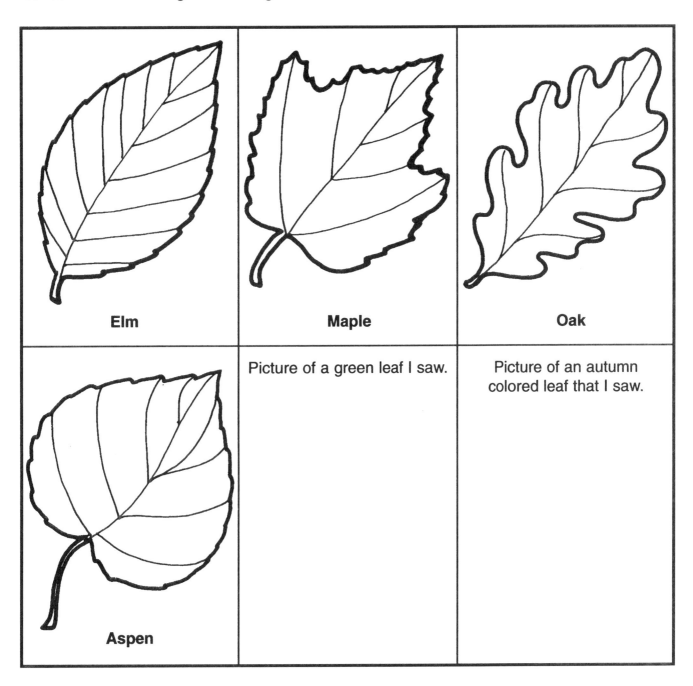

Elm	**Maple**	**Oak**
Aspen	Picture of a green leaf I saw.	Picture of an autumn colored leaf that I saw.

Instructions:

Go for a walk in a place with trees. Look for the leaves on the chart above. If you can, color the pictures here like the leaves that you saw.

Leaf Art

Make a Leaf Rubbing

Materials Needed: plain paper, leaves, crayons

Directions:

1. Find some pretty leaves.

2. Lay them underneath bond paper or recycled newsprint.

3. Press down on the paper with one hand and color firmly with a crayon in the other hand.

4. Lift the paper. You will see the outline of the leaf on the paper. Look closely for the veins of the leaf.

Pressing Leaves

Safety Note: An iron to be used only with adult supervision!

Materials Needed: large leaves; waxed paper; warm iron; small cotton towel or small brown paper bag; red, blue, or black construction paper

Directions:

1. Find some large leaves.

2. Put a leaf between two pieces of wax paper.

3. Place the towel or brown grocery bag over the wax paper and iron over the bag or cotton towel.

4. The wax will melt into the leaf to preserve it.

5. Make frames out of the construction paper. Glue or staple the leaves inside of the frames.

6. Use pressed leaf pictures for seasonal wall decorations.

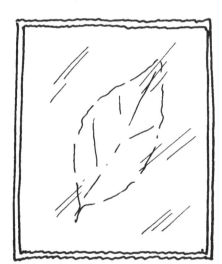

Make a Paper Tree with Real Leaves

Materials: large piece of brown construction paper, leaves fallen from trees, pencils, crayons, glue

Directions:

1. Draw the outline of a tree with no leaves on the construction paper.

2. Take the leaves and glue them to the branches of your paper tree.

Painting Pumpkins

Materials: three to five small, whole pumpkins; old newspapers; poster paints and brushes; extra decorations, such as small hats, etc.

Directions:

1. Put your pumpkins on newspapers.

2. Paint faces on your pumpkins, using **different** colors. Let one color dry before using another.

3. Add extra decorations for the way you want them to look.

4. Use these as a centerpiece or to decorate a shelf or window.

By using different sizes of pumpkins, you can make a family of pumpkins!

Put a Turkey Together

Materials: duplicate of this page on card stock or construction paper, crayons, colored pencils or markers, glue and scissors

Directions: Color, cut out, and assemble the pieces to make a Thanksgiving turkey. Glue head, feathers, and feet to the round body as shown in the example.

Autumn Vegetable People

Materials: duplicate of this page on card stock or white construction paper, craft sticks, crayons, colored pencils or markers, glue and scissors

Directions:

1. Color and cut out the autumn vegetable people.
2. Glue them to the craft sticks.
3. Put on a puppet show with your vegetable people.

Peanut Fun

Making Peanut People

Materials: peanuts in the shell, 2" x 5" (5 cm x 12.5 cm) pipe cleaners, colored markers, ball-point pen

Directions:

1. With the ballpoint pen, poke leg and arm holes in your peanut.
2. Push pipe cleaners through to make arms and legs.
3. With colored markers, draw faces and clothes on your peanut.
4. Arrange your peanut people into social groupings, such as a family or a school group. Show them doing something like having a picnic.

Peanut People Place

Materials: a shoe box, scissors, crayons, other small boxes

Directions:

1. Cut out one long side of the shoe box.
2. Draw a background, such as a living room in a house.
3. Use the small boxes to make furniture, such as tables, couches, etc.
4. Put the peanut people in the box.

Autumn Recipes

Safety Note: Cooking or heating should be done under close adult supervision.

Baked Pumpkin Seeds

Ingredients: two or three cups (500–750 mL) washed pumpkin seeds, one or two tablespoons (15–30 mL) of cooking oil, salt, paper towels

Directions:

1. Dry pumpkin seeds for one day on the paper towels.
2. Mix the seeds and oil together in a bowl.
3. Put them on a cookie sheet or in a pie pan and bake for 45 minutes at 350° F (180° C).
4. Sprinkle with salt for a healthy snack.

Autumn Punch

Ingredients: one quart (1 L) apple juice, one quart (1 L) orange juice, one quart (1 L) ginger ale, two whole oranges, ice

Directions:

1. Mix the juices and ginger ale together in a large bowl.
2. Cut up the oranges into slices and float them in the punch.
3. Serve with ice.

Warm Cider with Cinnamon

Ingredients: apple cider or juice, ground cinnamon

Directions:

1. Warm up cider or juice on the stove or in a crock pot.
2. Using a ladle or large spoon, pour it into mugs.
3. Sprinkle with cinnamon.

Pumpkin Face Cookies

Ingredients: large, round cookies, orange and black cake frosting in tubes, raisins, nuts, and chocolate chips

Directions:

1. Use the frosting to draw pumpkin faces on the cookies.
2. Make eyes, noses and mouths out of raisins, nuts or chocolate chips. These can be scary treats to eat!

Autumn Cards

Duplicate this page. Color and/or draw pictures. Cut out the cards. Give them to someone to help them remember that special day. In the last box design your own coupon.

My favorite football team:	A Leaf Bookmark	Happy Columbus Day!
_____		
Come watch the game with me on: _____	My favorite book:	
Signed: _____	_____	To:_____
	By: _____	From: _____
Happy Halloween!	Happy Thanksgiving!	Good for 1 free
		_____
To:_____	To:_____	To:_____
From: _____	From: _____	From: _____

Clip Art for Autumn

Welcome the season with a cornucopia of autumn colors. Decorate a section of a wall to help celebrate the season.

Directions: Make duplicates of this page on white bond or construction paper. Use the leaf clip art to make a border for the bulletin board. Copy, color, and cut out the leaves to make your own basketful of autumn colors. The leaves can also be glued to art tissue paper to make autumn wrapping paper.

Country Fair Clip Art

Harvest time means country fair time. A bounty of produce and many farm animals can be seen at the fair. Join in and celebrate by making a cut-out picture, using this Country Fair Clip Art.